C000154690

My Other Books On Amazon

UK Longshot Horse Racing System Paperback – 6 May 2021
https://www.amazon.co.uk/dp/B0948RPSHN

Most Profitable Horse Racing System Paperback – 16 Dec. 2020
https://www.amazon.co.uk/dp/B08QRB3CJY

Horse Racing Form Guide UK: Reading Horse Form Effectively Paperback – 26 Feb. 2021
https://www.amazon.co.uk/dp/B08XNBY89K

Best Horse Racing System Paperback – 10 May 2020
https://www.amazon.co.uk/dp/B088BF1CG7

Horse Racing System Seeing The Light Kindle Edition
https://www.amazon.co.uk/dp/B08LL4PWQP

Groupform UK Horse Racing System Kindle Edition
https://www.amazon.co.uk/dp/B084M4FSWN

Best Horse Racing System Kindle Edition
https://www.amazon.co.uk/dp/B084V9S4Z7

Picking Winners No Problem: Horse Racing Betting System Kindle Edition
https://www.amazon.co.uk/dp/B08BJXMN3R

UK Horse Racing Handicap System: Took 2 Years To Computer Model Kindle Edition
https://www.amazon.co.uk/dp/B084VRDL8T

Betfair Place Market UK Horse Handicap System: Horse Racing Betting System Kindle Edition
https://www.amazon.co.uk/dp/B089FHPSM7

Horse Racing Betting Secret System: UK Horse Racing System To Change Your Betting Kindle Edition
https://www.amazon.co.uk/dp/B08CVSZW39

UK Professional Horse Racing Betting Edge Kindle Edition
https://www.amazon.co.uk/dp/B08JM3FV4M

Horse Racing Betting Dutching System Kindle Edition
https://www.amazon.co.uk/dp/B08BDN5VGK

The 6f 7f Furlong Hope Horse Lay System Simple To Use And Profitable Kindle Edition
https://www.amazon.co.uk/dp/B084RHCCSX

How To Implement Your Own UK Racing System

Introduction

This is not as easy as you think and it took me quite some time to implement a UK horse racing handicap system that worked automatically on a daily basis. During my journey there were many times I wish I had never started the project. I had over 25 years of I.T. experience in SQL, Unix and relational database technologies and I thought it would be a stroll in the park! How wrong I was I had underestimated how large and the number of tasks that would be involved in the implementation of this automatic UK horse racing handicap system.

This book covers all aspects of this implementation including the algorithm that is used in the horse racing system to pick winning horse selections in UK handicap horse races automatically. When I say automatic what I mean by this is when the horse racing system is run a small selection of horses would be produced that could qualify as potential bets. With this in mind I would say the horse UK racing system was 95% automatic which is pretty good. How long would it take to trawl through horse form for every horse in every race!

I wrote this book to help punters create a similar automatic UK horse racing handicap system that works and explain the pitfalls so they can implement it quicker and more smoothly. You will need to be an existing punter who has the basic understanding of UK horse form and an above average understanding of computers.

Implementing a decent UK horse racing system cannot be achieved in days it's more like months so be prepared to put some hard work into its implementation. An alternate solution is to outsource the work but this will cost quite a large amount of money. You will learn more implementing it yourself and gain some satisfaction from your labours.

I really hope you enjoy this book and implement your UK horse racing handicap system successfully and more importantly profit from the system on a daily basis.

Where Do We Start?

When implementing an automatic UK horse racing handicap system you need to outline all the high level key components of the system in terms of,

- Technology to be used in terms of software and hardware.
- Horse past results data source.
- Horse racing current declarations.
- Horse racing system algorithm.
- Horse selection reporting picking potential winning horses.
- Securing your database.

Once you have the above list you can start adding more detail to these high level components of your intended racing UK horse racing handicap system. We will cover each of these high level components in more detail in the book.

A word of caution it is better to spend time flushing out the detail of the high level components as the further you go down the road of implementing your system you do not want to realise you got the design wrong. We call this rework and it is very expensive in terms of time and money. When I was an I.T. freelance consultant a great deal of emphasis was placed on capturing functional requirements at a business level from the start and then implementing a high level design around this. If the design is too complicated it will fail, the high level design should meet the business requirements nothing more and nothing less. It is better to deliver these business requirements on time and working rather than fail because you were over ambitious or misunderstood the business requirements.

The old saying the devil is in the detail and how true this is!

Prototyping Your Implementation

This is how I started my implementation as I had a great deal of free time at night in hotels when I was a freelance computer consultant. I also performed prototyping whilst on train journeys or whenever I had free time outside normal working hours. In fact it actually became addictive sometimes I would be at breakfast in my hotel running prototypes.

The prototyping allowed me to identify potential problems earlier in the design so I could combat these before I was too far down the implementation cycle.

What did prototyping identify?

It was mainly ironing out the horses past results data and current race data formats what they looked like from the external data source I was paying for like the excellent Raceform Interactive software.

1. Identifying horse form data source formats i.e. a horses weight of a 9-11 which is 9 stone 11 pounds would have to be converted to total weight in pounds to make processing easier.

2. A horses name had a country code like **(IRE)** e.g. a horse name **Claim The Stars (IRE)** so I needed to strip this country code from the horse's name. Please see code snipper how I achieved this using SQL –Structured Query Language.

/**** Start Of SQL Code Snippet**

```
select distinct speed, hand, sp_char, master_hurdle_rating, master_chase_rating,
trainer,jockey,master_adjusted_rating,master_unadjusted_rating,race_type,race_date,race_time,race_number,replace(replace(replace(replace(replace(replace(replace(replace(replace(replace(replace
(replace(replace(replace(replace(replace(replace(replace(horse, '(IRE)',
''),'(FR)',''),'(NZ)',''),'(GER)', ''),'(USA)',''),'(ARG)', ''),'(BEL)', ''),'(UAE)', ''), '(POL)', ''),'(BRZ)', ''), '(SWI)',
''), '(SWE)', ''), '(JPN)', ''), '(AUS)', ''), '(HOL)', ''), '(SAF)', ''), '(SLO)', ''),'(CAN)', ''),'(GR)', '') as
horse,class,distance,course,going,weight,jock_club_rating,jock_allow,age,prize  from
generic.curr_decs where race_type in ('FLT', 'AWF', 'FLT') and hand in ( '0', '1' )  order by
race_date,course,race_time, horse
```

/**** End Of SQL Code Snippet**

3. Horse form data types and lengths i.e. horse name, jockey, trainer, course, going and many more. An example of this is the course data entity length 40 or 50 characters etc to store this data entity. These were some of the details that needed to be identified early in the implementation.
4. Prototyping also allowed me to identify key data entities earlier in the horse form data source such as was the race a handicap or non handicap. Was the race a flat or all weather race and many more.

I like prototyping as long it does not cost me financially. I was able to load past horse form data and current horse racing declarations into simple database tables and iron out any data problems early in the implementation cycle.

I thoroughly recommend you adopt this prototyping approach when implementing your horse racing system. I approximately spent a month prototyping and I will not lie it was hard work and quite frustrating. When I say it took a month by the end of this period I had only loaded 1 year's UK past horse race results into my database table **Past Results Table.** I also loaded a number of weeks UK current horse declarations into my database table **Today's Horse Racing Declaration Table.**

During this first month I was constantly adding more and more horse form data entities to these two tables. I was also prototyping horse racing selections those that would be possible bets. I soon realised to make any realistic predictions of winning horses I would have to load 10 years of past results into the **Past Results Table.** By the end of this prototyping my two tables looked like below,

```sql
CREATE TABLE "Past_Results_Table" (
        "HORSE" CHAR(50 OCTETS) NOT NULL ,
        "AGE" INTEGER ,
        "COURSE" VARCHAR(50 OCTETS) NOT NULL ,
        "GOING" CHAR(5 OCTETS) ,
        "GOING_ALLOWANCE" CHAR(10 OCTETS) ,
        "CUMULATIVE_LENGTH_BEATEN" CHAR(10 OCTETS) ,
        "MEDIAN_TIME" CHAR(10 OCTETS) ,
        "POSITION" CHAR(3 OCTETS) ,
        "RACE_DATE" DATE NOT NULL ,
        "DISTANCE" CHAR(10 OCTETS) ,
        "RACE_TYPE" CHAR(10 OCTETS) ,
        "RACE_NUMBER" CHAR(5 OCTETS) ,
        "RACEFORM_RATING" INTEGER ,
        "SP" CHAR(10 OCTETS) ,
        "SIRE" CHAR(50 OCTETS) ,
        "TRACK_TYPE" CHAR(10 OCTETS) ,
        "WEIGHT" CHAR(8 OCTETS) ,
        "WINNER_TIME" CHAR(15 OCTETS) ,
        "BHB" CHAR(5 OCTETS) ,
        "CLASS" CHAR(5 OCTETS) ,
        "YEAR" CHAR(5 OCTETS) ,
        "PREV_RUNS" INTEGER ,
        "PATTERN" CHAR(3 OCTETS) ,
        "PRIZE1" CHAR(8 OCTETS) ,
        "TRAINER" VARCHAR(100 OCTETS) ,
        "JOCKEY" VARCHAR(100 OCTETS) ,
        "SPEED" INTEGER ,
        "FAV" VARCHAR(2 OCTETS) WITH DEFAULT ' ' ,
        "HAND" VARCHAR(5 OCTETS) WITH DEFAULT ' ' )
    COMPRESS YES ADAPTIVE
    IN "USERSPACE1"


CREATE TABLE "Todays_Horse_Racing_Declaration_Table " (
        "COURSE" VARCHAR(50 OCTETS) ,
        "RACE_DATE" DATE ,
        "RACE_TIME" CHAR(5 OCTETS) ,
        "RACE_NUMBER" CHAR(5 OCTETS) ,
        "CLASS" CHAR(5 OCTETS) ,
        "DISTANCE" CHAR(10 OCTETS) ,
        "HORSE" CHAR(50 OCTETS) ,
        "MASTER_CHASE_RATING" INTEGER ,
        "MASTER_HURDLE_RATING" INTEGER ,
        "MASTER_ADJUSTED_RATING" INTEGER ,
```

```
"MASTER_UNADJUSTED_RATING" INTEGER ,
"MEDIAN_TIME" CHAR(20 OCTETS) ,
"RACE_TYPE" CHAR(10 OCTETS) ,
"WEIGHT" CHAR(10 OCTETS) ,
"GOING" CHAR(5 OCTETS) ,
"JOCK_CLUB_RATING" CHAR(5 OCTETS) ,
"JOCK_ALLOW" INTEGER ,
"RACE_TITLE" VARCHAR(250 OCTETS) ,
"AGE" INTEGER ,
"DAYS_LAST_RUN" INTEGER ,
"PRIZE" INTEGER ,
"SPEED" CHAR(8 OCTETS) ,
"TRAINER" VARCHAR(100 OCTETS) ,
"JOCKEY" VARCHAR(100 OCTETS) ,
"HAND" CHAR(1 OCTETS) ,
"SP_CHAR" CHAR(10 OCTETS) )
IN "USERSPACE1"
```

This was a crude database physical model as there were two driving tables with no real entity relationship modelling but it was well indexed and it was pretty fast in processing 10 years past horse form data on a daily basis. We will delve deeper into the implementation of the racing system I still use today after many years. I have never really changed this implementation but I certainly have used these database tables to model different horse racing systems effectively. This is the beauty of this is that you can data mine and it does throw some useful patterns which help you pick winning horses. My horse racing system only looks at UK handicap horse racing as I love solving this puzzle. You can also develop non handicap horse racing systems it is up to you.

So Which High Level Component Do We Start With First?

In my opinion it is the **horse past result data source** and **current declarations data source** are the key to your horse racing system. I will explain in more detail later in this book. Basically without clean, accurate and up to date horse past results data your horse racing system will produce rubbish, remember **GIGO** garbage in garbage out! You also have to consider what horse form data you are going to need and how you will capture this data. Lastly you will need to consider what format the data is in and whether you will have to clean and transform and aggregate this data. Designing a data store or database for this data is not technically demanding but it does require thought in terms of how much data you will be storing and how often you update this data and very importantly how you secure this data.

In my opinion this is one of the key areas of a horse racing system and once this is correct querying or data mining the data is straightforward. You can slice and dice data very easily using bespoke reporting or by tools that will interface with your data easily.

I will not pretend here you will certainly have to pay for a data source this data does not come free. There is screen scraping to obtain data but whether this is legal I would not know, you might have to ask the data source provider for permission. One other problem of screen scraping is that the format of screens change over a period of time so one day your horse racing system might not work.

Understanding UK Horse Past Results Data

When I started prototyping UK jump races or national hunt racing I looked at one race in terms of the data I would need now but also for the future. If we expand on this area more we can immediately say we need the following horse form data entities.

Horse Form Data Entity

Horse Name
Age
Weight
Position
Course
Distance
Total Wins For This Horse
Total Places For This Horse

Now if we were to use the above data entities for our horse racing system we would not get far. This data is too broad and it does not really indicate what a horse's ability or class is. Ok it does indicate how many wins the horse has had and how many times the horse was placed. But what was the race penalty value (race prize money) and class of races did it win or was placed in they are the next questions we ask ourselves.

So we will add to our horse form data entities as follows,

Horse Form Data Entity

Horse Name
Age
Weight
Position
Course
Distance
Total Wins For This Horse
Total Places For This Horse
Class Of Race
Race Penalty Value (Race Prize Money)

So we now know the class of race the horse won or was placed in and the penalty value of the race this being the race prize money. The class of race could be a class 3 or class 6 or Group race etc. It goes to say that the best horses compete in races with greater prize money. We also have the distance and course and importantly the weight the horse was carrying in the race.

But ten horse form data entities are still not enough and we will need a great deal more information if we are to move forward with the implementation.

When we download and extract our horse past results data from our external data source we will need to transform some of this data I will give you an example of this. Our data source will not contain all the horse form data entities we need like the number of times a horse has won at a particular course or distance etc. There are many more derived data entities like class wins and class places.

An interesting data entity would be how many races a horse has won over a certain race distance like 2 miles. So we would have to query our extracted data and calculate this value and call it data entity distance wins.

Horse Form Data Entity

Horse Name
Age
Total Wins For This Horse
Total Places For This Horse
Class Of Race
Race Penalty Value
Distance Wins

We could extend the above data entity list further by adding the number of course wins for a horse and then take this further with course places.

Horse Form Data Entity

Horse Name
Age
Total Wins For This Horse
Total Places For This Horse
Class Of Race
Race Penalty Value
Distance Wins
Course Wins
Course Places

Let's be adventurous and add going wins and weight wins and total runs for a horse in its racing career. The data entity total runs the number of races a horse has competed in.

Horse Form Data Entity

Horse Name
Age
Total Wins For This Horse
Total Places For This Horse
Class Of Race
Race Penalty Value
Distance Wins
Course Wins
Course Places
Going Wins
Weight Wins
Total Runs

Our data entity weight wins indicates how many races a horse has won with a particular weight.

We will delve deeper into data entities later in the book.

So we have two types of data entities,

1. Data received from the horse past result data source this is the raw data that is normally paid for and downloaded via an extract file comma delimited.
2. Derived data is the data we calculate from the raw data in 1 above like 'distance wins' for a horse plus many more.

We now need to look at how much horse past results data we need to start with for example 1 year or 2 years or 5 years or 10 years, I went with 10 years. My database started with an initial 10 years of horse past results data so this involved importing or loading the raw data for 10 years into my database table Past_Results_Table i.e. all the races a horse has competed in terms of course, race position, weight and distance and many more. This process I call the initial refresh of past results data that will be added to every 'N' number of days via past results data deltas.

The next step was to refresh this data in other words keep the database up to date with horses latest runs so I opted for a strategy of every 5 days. I would refresh and apply a horse past result data delta to the main database we will discuss this later in more detail. This delta contained all the latest races horses had won in over the last 5 days. So my database was never more than 5 days old. It is important to keep your database current as your racing system cannot work on old and stale data.

Technology Required To Implement Your UK Horse Racing System

Most laptops and desktop computers are more than powerful enough to implement and run a horse racing system. I use a basic desktop worth £900 with twin monitors and this processes the horse form data quickly. It can produce horse selections for a day's UK horse racing in 30 seconds. Unless you intend to do this commercially I would not invest in state of the art computers for this.

The hardware side of the horse racing system implementation is easy the next is what operating systems we use to implement it. When I started on my journey developing my racing system the answer was straight forward. I would use Microsoft windows version 10 as the main operating system with VMware virtual partition for an Ubuntu Unix operating system. Below is a download link for VMware software which is free.

https://www.vmware.com/uk/products/workstation-player.html

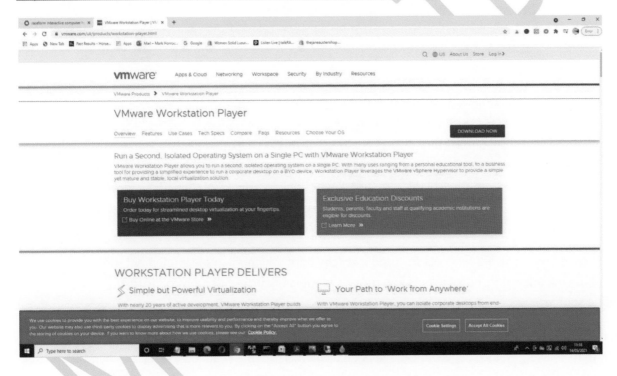

Microsoft windows would be used to download the horse form data extracts and Ubuntu for the horse past results database and horse racing system selection processing. Ubuntu is a version of the Unix operating system which I have 20+ years experience of using plus I wanted my database to exist on Unix as I am more comfortable with this and it is easier to navigate for me.

Ubuntu is open-source and is free to download. This Unix operating system and it's tools are very powerful so this made my implementation a great deal easier. I included a download link below and it is free software.

https://ubuntu.com/download/desktop

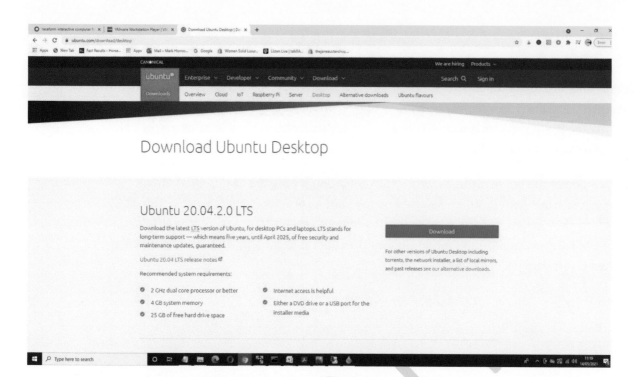

The downloaded and extracted past horse results and current horse declarations files that exist on the Microsoft windows operating system could easily be accessed from the Ubuntu Unix operating system using a mounted file system. So when horse form data extract files were downloaded to Microsoft Windows 10 folders or directories these could be cleaned and loaded into the database tables that resided on Ubuntu operating system. This is possible as Microsoft Windows 10 folders or directories can be mounted from Ubuntu this was a major technology win, key to my horse racing implementation. Once past horse results data extracts had been downloaded to Microsoft Windows 10 folders they could easily be processed in the Ubuntu operating system.

I am not a keen fan of Microsoft windows so I used it for the bare minimum in the implementation it was used for downloading past horse results and today's runners or current declaration from my external data source which I will outline later.

So you may ask where was the source of my past horse results data, well I only use one excellent source and that is Raceform Interactive and I have been using this for 10 + years they offer excellent support and is very good value. I left a link below so you can look at the features etc.

https://raceforminteractive.com/raceform-interactive

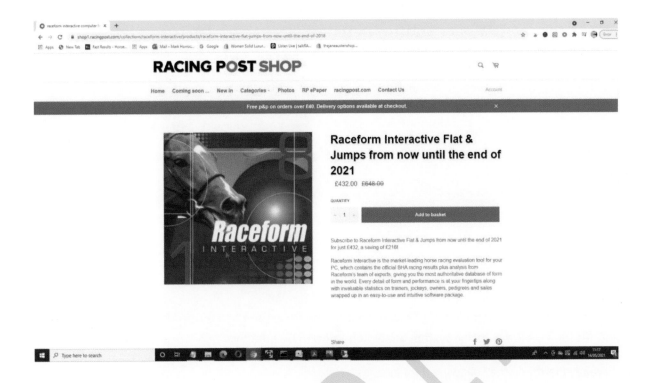

I thoroughly recommend it. This is a paid for data source and is relatively cheap approximately £700 for the year.

So to summaries the technology I use for my UK horse racing system is as follows,

Hardware

Desktop with twin monitors

Software

Microsoft windows 10 Operating

VMware workstation player   https://www.vmware.com/uk/products/workstation-player.html

Ubuntu Unix Operating System   https://ubuntu.com/download/desktop

Raceform Interactive   https://raceforminteractive.com/raceform-interactive

You need to install VMware workstation player software on your Microsoft Windows 10 Operating System and then create a virtual partition where you install the Ubuntu Unix opertaing system. This is quite easy to implement and it is just a matter of doing some reading and leg work. You could always pay to have this implemented but its more rewarding doing it yourself.

We now have our technology to implement our UK horse racing system now we need to look more at the database and its data entities and the bespoke software that will generate our horse racing selections automatically and winning bets!

Horse Form Database And Data Entities In Detail

In this chapter I want to discuss data entities that our UK horse racing system will use in its implementation in more detail. These data entities will then be allocated into 3 groups below,

1. Past Horse Race Results
2. Current Declarations (Race Card)
3. Derived Data

We touched on this earlier but we need to put more meat on the bone here as we need more horse form data entities for a UK horse racing system implementation to be effective.

So we have already identified the following data entities below.

Horse Form Data Entity

Horse Name
Age
Total Wins For This Horse
Total Places For This Horse
Class Of Race
Race Penalty Value
Distance Wins
Course Wins
Course Places
Going Wins
Weight Wins
Total Runs

We need to add data entities race date, course, going, last race position, the horse BHB rating and number of days the horse last ran.

Horse Form Data Entity

Horse Name
Age
Total Wins For This Horse
Total Places For This Horse
Class Of Race
Race Penalty Value (Prize Money)

Distance Wins
Course Wins
Course Places
Going Wins
Weight Wins
Total Runs
Last Race Position
BHB rating
Days Last Run
Course
Going
Race Date

Now let's look at allocating the above data entities to our 3 groups mentioned earlier.

1. **Past Horse Race Results**

Race Date
Course
Going
Horse Name
Age
Weight
Distance
Race Penalty Value (Prize Money)
Last Race Position
BHB rating

The above are the basic data entities we need for our horse past results table in our database. I have racing systems that use many more entities but this is a good starting point.

Derived Data Entities

Total Wins For This Horse
Total Places For This Horse
Distance Wins
Course Wins
Course Places
Going Wins
Weight Wins
Total Runs
Days Last Run

Horse Form Consistency Value
Average Ability For The Horse

The history and derived data entities are still not enough to implement our horse racing system. We need the horse data for the current day's races i.e. the race card. I shall refer to this as current declarations. These current declarations are normally downloaded and extracted from our external data source the night before racing starts or on the day of racing.
This extract is downloaded to a folder or directory under Microsoft Windows 10 and is visible to the Ubuntu Unix operating system for processing.

So what horse from data entities do we need for current declarations we certainly need course, race time and horse.

Current Declarations Data Entities

Course
Race Time
Horse

We really need more data than just the 3 data entities we need the weight the horse is carrying, distance of the race and the horses BHB rating. I have also added race type and if it's a handicap race.

Current Declarations Data Entities

Race Date
Course
Race Time
Distance
Horse
Weight
BHB Rating
Race Type (FLT/NH/AWF)
Handicap Race (Y/N)
Jockey
Trainer

I also include jockey and trainer data entities for current declarations for analysis when modelling past horse races.

I have not included any speed ratings in the **Current Declarations Data Entities**
As my horse racing systems do not use these I personally think too much emphasis is put on speed figures but that is my opinion.

We have made great progress we have identified the horse data entities we need and what data is current, historic and derived.

- **Current Declarations Data Entities (Today's Races)**
- **Derived Data Entities (Derived From Historic Data)**
- **History Data Entities (Past Race Results Of The Horses)**

Now we need to allocate data types and lengths to these data entities whether they are current, derived or history as we will need this when we create database tables to store this data.

Horse Form Data Entity Types

When we store data in database tables we need to understand what type of data we are storing. An example of this: do we use an integer for the horse's age rather than characters for a horse's age etc. Types of data are important for storage cost and processing speed and more importantly for querying our data in the database tables. Below are example SQL queries to retrieve horse data whose age is 9 one query using integer and the other using characters predicates.

Select horse, age from current declarations table where age = '9' ←------ String

Or

Select horse, age from current declarations table where age = 9 ←------ Numeric

Is the data entity Age to be stored as a numeric or as a character string?

You could store it as a string and covert to a numeric later but it is easier just to store it as a numeric. You need to ensure you understand your data to avoid loading or importing data errors, data cannot be loaded into wrong data types i.e. character string into a numeric etc.

This is where prototyping helped me immensely I downloaded sample horse past results data extracts from my external data source Raceform Interactive and examined its contents and lengths and then mapped data types and length to each field (data entity) in the data extracts.

As mentioned earlier I use the excellent Raceform Interactive as my paid for external data source. This tool has an excellent past horse race results and current declarations data export utility. I was able to export this data and then determine the data types and lengths to be used. Once I achieved this I could create my database tables at physical model level.

So let's flush out the data types for **History Data Entities (Past Race Results Of The Horses)** using Raceform Interactive.

Using Raceform Interactive To Download Past Results And Race Card Data

Downloading This Data

The blue line on the screenshot below is where you download the overnight current declarations you simple tick the box **'Overnights'** and click on the **'Connect'** button pointed to in red. You can download the past horse race results by ticking the box **'Update to latest'** pointed to in green and click on **'Connect'** button pointed to in red. This data is loaded into Raceform Interactive database held on your computer the next step is to export these past horse results and current declaration data to a comma delimited file ready for processing.

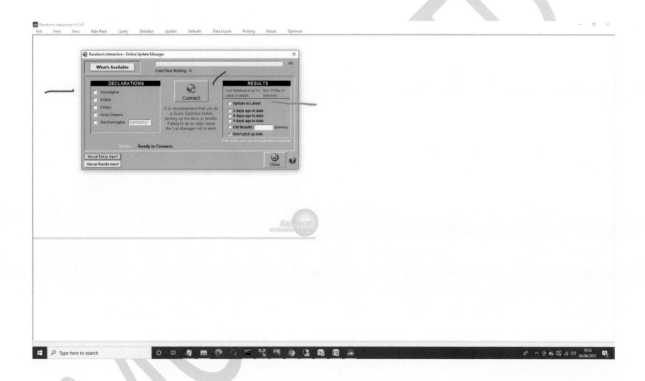

We can now extract the past horse results data using the screenshot below. The vertical blue line identifies the data entity values we want to export to a comma delimited file on our computer. The red line points to the months and year of the past results data we want to export. So in this example we are only interested in data entity values for year 2021 and the month May. You can save this query for later use when you want to export past results deltas obviously you will have to change your year and month values pointed to by the red line.

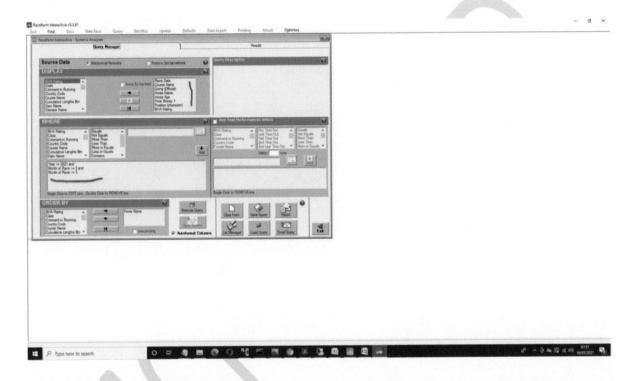

To export this data you simply click on the **'Export Results'** button pointed to by the blue line on the screenshot below.

In the above screenshot you can see the results list is 144347 records for year 2019. We would hit the button 'Export Results'.

Below is a data extract screenshot with a smaller results list 6132 records. You simply enter a filename and the past results data extract will be written to a comma delimited file with that filename which you can use to load into your database tables or Excel spreadsheet on your computer.

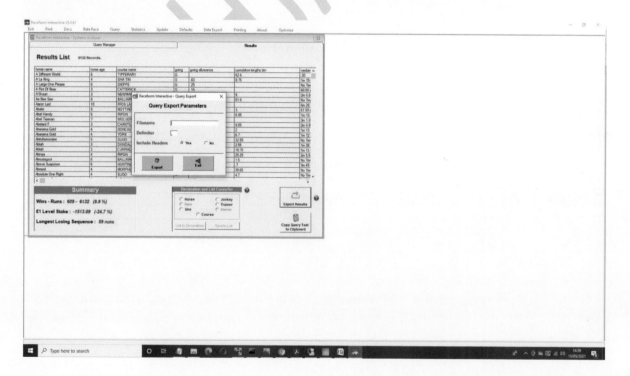

The past results data extract will be written to the file **'past results'** on your computer.

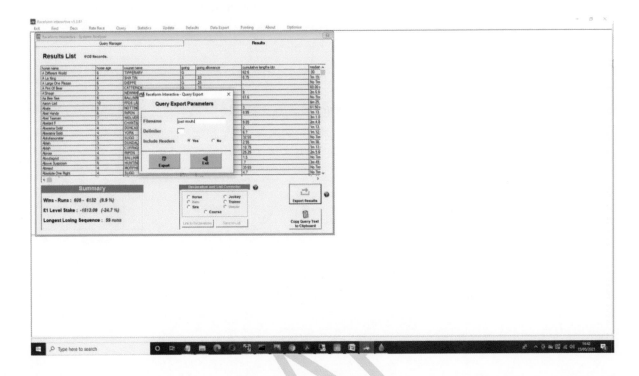

You can see by the blue line in the screenshot below the past results data extract has been created successfully and written to the Raceform Interactive folder (directory).

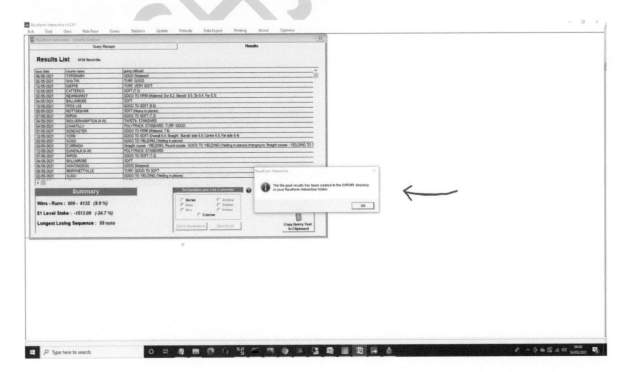

You can see from the screenshot below the past results data extract has been written to a directory on your computer which you set in the Raceform Interactive settings.

The past results data extract will be written to a directory or folder on your computer under the default directory **C:\RaceformData** you can change this directory in the Raceform Interactive settings see screenshots below and the setting pointed to by the black line.

You can see from the screenshot below the export file has been exported to a directory on your computer pointed to in red and you can see the filename **'past results'** pointed to by blue.

All my exported data files from Raceform Interactive are written to the directory or folder below,

C:\Raceform\export

You can see the file **'Past Results'** export file in the directory **C:\Raceform\export**

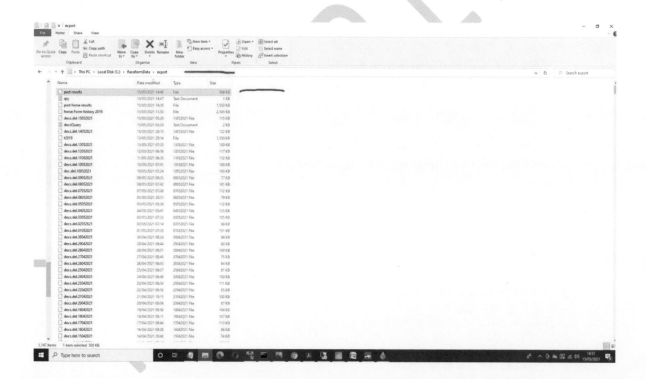

There are many other settings you can change in the Raceform Interactive settings screen.

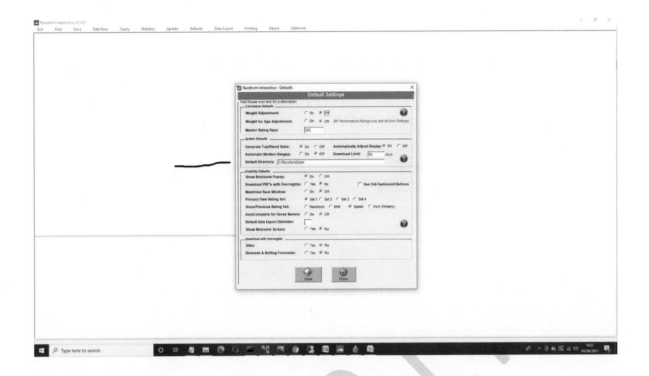

If we take a look at the first 5 records of the file 'past results' below we can see our past results data extract. When building your database and tables you will have to initially load all the historical data for N number of years into these tables. The number of years of past horse form data you load should be more than 5 years to ensure you have enough history for an effective UK horse racing handicap system.

Loading this historical data will take time but it is important you get it right with no missing data or gaps for the horses in your database.

'past results' file

race date	course name	going (official)	horse name	horse age	prize	position	bhb rating
06/05/2021	TIPPERARY	GOOD (Watered)	A Different World	6	£5,795	15	97
02/05/2021	SHA TIN	TURF: GOOD	A La King	4	£53,824	11	60
10/05/2021	CATTERICK	SOFT (7.3)	A Pint Of Bear	3	£4,347	1	75
08/05/2021	NOTTINGHAM	SOFT (Heavy in places)	Abate	5	£4,347	3	76
07/05/2021	RIPON	GOOD TO SOFT (7.2)	Abel Handy	6	£5,234	9	84

So we can derive data entities from this historical data as mentioned earlier like the total runs a horse has had by simply querying or data mining this historical data in our database tables. I use **SQL – Structure Query Language** to query my database tables. So a simple query below would derive the total runs data entity as follows,

Select count(*) as total runs from past history table where horse = 'A Pint Of Bear'

We could also derive the data entity total wins for a horse as follows,

Select count(*) as total wins from past horse results table where horse = 'A Pint Of Bear' and position=1

We could also derive the data entity total prize money won for a horse as follows,

Select sum total prize money from past horse results table where horse = 'A Pint Of Bear' and position=1

These are just a few examples of derived horse form data entities and there are many more.

I have deliberately left out one key data entity from the past results data and that is **race distance** when I was building my historical database I would suddenly realise I need another data entity like jockey weight claim. So it is important to determine as earlier as possible in the design to identify all the data entities you require that will need to be downloaded from Raceform Interactive. The race distance data entity is quite important for any horse racing system implementation for obvious reasons.

Past Results Data Types

From the above sample data extract file **'past results'** we now know what our data looks like so we need to assign data types to this data in order to build our database and tables. I use a relational database which contains a simple logical and physical data model. This data model uses tables to store the data for our horse racing system.

Below is our database table definition to store our past results extract data. As you can see it is very simple but effective.

Past Results Table

Data Entity	Data Type	Length
Race Date	Date	4
Course	Character	50
Going	Going	25
Horse Name	Character	50
Age	Integer	4
Prize1	Character	8
Last Race Position	Character	3
BHB Rating	Character	5
Race Distance	Character	10
Last Weight	Character	10

So we now have our past horse results data defined and our database table which we will need to load our past results data into. As mentioned earlier we can derive a great deal of useful data entities from this historical data like total runs, distance wins, course wins and a horse's current consistency form by adding up the positions from the horses last 3 races.

You have so much data mining power with this one historical results table, the more data entities this table contains like trainer, jockey etc the more you can derive from it.

Today's Horse Racing Declaration Data Entities

We will need the current horse declarations for the current days racing, these are normally found on the race card in the Racing Post website but I download this from Raceform Interactive. I will touch on the third type of data required these being derived data entities later on.

Below shows a screenshot and the keys areas are highlighted with a blue line. I use the excellent Raceform Interactive software to download today's horse racing data (race card) and load into our database.

This follows the same process for downloading past history horse data to an export file explained earlier in the book.

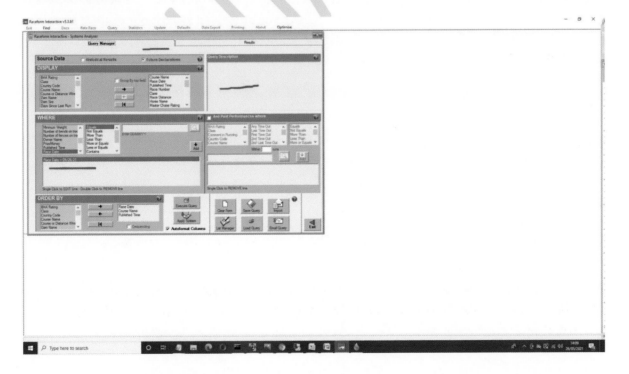

We simply click on the **'Export Results'** button in the screenshot below. This data will be exported in comma delimited format. This means each column data is separated by a comma for easier processing. I have highlighted with a blue line how many records **517** will be exported in the screenshot below for the given date of **26th May 2021**.

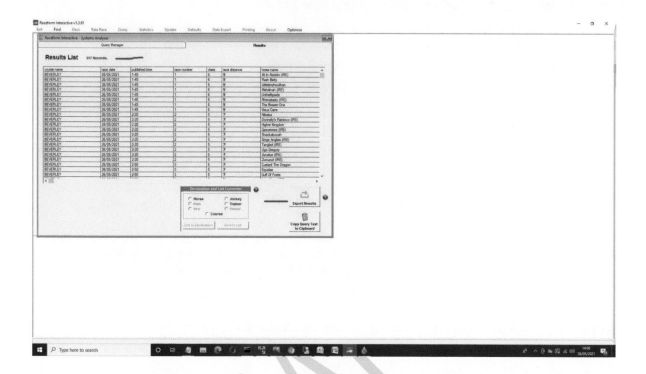

Once we have obtained the exported comma delimited file we need to define the data types for the data entities as we did for the past results table. I have outlined these types for our new table below. This table will hold our current declaration data i.e. today's races to be processed against our past results tables. These two database tables will form the basis of our horse form data store for our UK horse racing handicap system.

Today's Horse Racing Declaration Table

Data Entity	Data Type	Length
Race Date	Date	4
Todays Course	Character	50
Race Time	Character	5
Going	Going	25
Horse Name	Character	50
Age	Integer	4
Prize1	Character	8
BHB Rating	Character	5
Todays Race Distance	Character	10
Jockey	Character	100
Trainer	Character	100
Race Type	Character	10

Hand	Character	1
Todays Weight	Character	10
Class Of Race	Character	5
Days Horse Last Run	Integer	4

The data entity **'Hand'** indicates whether the race is a handicap or not. The data entity **'Race Type'** indicates what type of race it is i.e. AWF or FLT etc

Derived Data Entities

Using our past result table described above we will now derive useful horse form data entities that are invaluable in implementing a UK horse racing handicap system.

We are interested in the following derived values,

Total runs for a horse
Distance wins for a horse
Ability for a horse
Course wins for a horse
Horse form consistency value (The sum of the last 3 race positions).

Below are examples of SQL – Structured Query Language queries to obtain this derived data.

1. Total runs for a horse

Select count(*) as total runs from past history table where horse = 'A Pint Of Bear'

2. Distance wins for a horse

Select count(*) as distance wins from past history table, current decs table where horse = 'A Pint Of Bear' and Race Distance = Todays Race Distance and Last Race Position='1'

3. Ability for a horse (In average winning prize money won).

Select sum(Prize1) as ability from past_history_table where horse = 'A Pint Of Bear' and Last Race Position='1'

We could then divide this value of total winning prize money prize1 by the total number of races the horse won to give us a value of average winning prize money for the horse. This would give us the average ability of the horse in terms of the average prize money the horse has won in its career. This derived value is a very good yardstick in assessing horse form i.e. does the horse have the ability to win a race.

4. Course wins for a horse

Select count(*) as course wins from past history table, current decs table where horse = 'A Pint Of Bear' and course=Todays Course and Last Race Position='1'

5. Horse form consistency value

Select last race position from past history table where horse = 'A Pint Of Bear' order by race date desc fetch first 3 rows only

The above SQL statement would fetch the last race positions for the horse latest race dates.
We then can add up these 3 race positions and use this as a horse form consistency value. This is another useful derived data entity in assessing horse form in terms of how consistent the horse is.

Example

Race Date   Last race Position
24/11/2020 1
10/11/2020 4
08/07/2020 2

horse form consistency value = **1+4+2 = 7**

If the last race position was **'UR'** unseated rider you could assign a value of **10**. The value you assign for non numeric last race positions is up to you.

The 3 Database Tables

We now have 3 database tables below which we can use to implement the main part of our UK horse racing handicap system.

Past Results Table

Today's Horse Racing Declaration Table

Derived Data Table

Let's recap on what we have learned from previous chapters.

Step 1

Load horse racing results past data into our table **Past Results Table.**

This will consist of an initial load of past years data say up to 2010 this is a one-off task.

This will have to be refreshed at regular intervals as data deltas to this **Past Results Table.** I do this refresh every **5 days** to keep the database up to date.

Step 2 Daily Task

We need to load the current racing declarations into the **Today's Horse Racing Declaration Table** this is the data for today's racing you will run the horse racing system using this data. This data has to be downloaded on a daily basis if you intend to run your UK horse racing handicap system every day.

Step 3 Daily Task

The Derived Data database Table is populated on a daily basis when running your UK horse racing system. This table is important for selecting the correct horses to place your bets on. In the next chapter I will walk you through the algorithm for a particular horse UK racing handicap system I use for handicap races only. This uses minimal derived data entities as above and current horse declaration data from the **Today's Horse Racing Declaration Table.**

UK Horse Racing Handicap System Algorithm That Works.

We save the best to the last but we needed to establish the technological framework to achieve a winning UK horse racing handicap system.

Before we delve into this once you have this technology framework you can model many horse racing systems and test these on past racing results. This has proved very effective for me over the years. I have prototyped 100's of UK handicap horse racing systems and non handicap ones as well.

Summary Of The Horse Racing Selection Algorithm

Below is the high level functional decomposition of this horse racing algorithm using our 3 database tables described earlier. This is used for UK handicap horse races only and it works very well indeed.

The following 5 functional components of our horse racing algorithm can be easily implemented using our 3 database tables.

1. Number of days the horse ran its last race is less than or equal to 50 days.
2. The horse has won at today's race distance.
3. The racing weight difference from its last race and today's race is less than or equal to 0.
4. The horse's Horse form consistency value is in the top 3 ranking for today's race.
5. The horse last race prize money is in the top 3 ranking for today's race.
6. The average ability is in the top 4 ranking for today's race.

The above is so simple to automate once the 3 database tables are populated with data.

Let's take each functional component above and explain the implementation in detail using our 3 database tables.

1. **Number of days since the horse ran its last race is less than or equal to 50 days.**

The stored procedure or SQL code snippet below is actual code taken from my UK Horse racing handicap system it is used to derive the number of days a horse last run. There is probably more efficient ways to write this SQL but I did write this code in 2010 in my spare time normally on trains or in cafes!

/**** Start Of SQL Code Snippet**

```
CREATE PROCEDURE hr.get_days_flt(IN_COURSE VARCHAR(50), IN IN_RACE_TIME

CHAR(5), IN_HORSE VARCHAR(50), IN IN_RACE_DATE DATE )

DYNAMIC RESULT SETS 1

BEGIN


DECLARE IT_COUNT integer;--
DECLARE v_date date;--

for A1 as
    select distinct(race_date) as c_date from Today's Horse Racing Declaration Table
do
    set v_date = c_date;--
end for;--

for P1 as
    select (days(v_date) - days(max(race_date))) as dayslr from Past Results Table where upper(IN_HORSE)
= upper(horse) and race_date < IN_RACE_DATE
do

        update generic.dumtab_flt set = P1.dayslr where horse = IN_HORSE and race_date =
IN_RACE_DATE;--

end for;--

END;
```

Note: The table **generic.dumtab_flt** is our derived data table used for reporting later i.e. to obtain possible horse selections that qualify as best bets, this table is cleared down for every days racing.

You will notice the **_flt** at the end of the table name as this denotes flat racing. I have two separate tables for (flt, AWF) and Jumps racing this makes processing easier.

We can see our data entity **days_last_run** P1.dayslr will store the number of days the horse ran its last race.

The parameter **IN_RACE_DATE** is the race day we want to process i.e. today's races etc taken from the **Today's Horse Racing Declaration Table.**

We are now on our way to implementing our UK horse racing handicap system.

2. **The horse has won at today's race distance.**

This is another easy data entity to derive from your **Past Results Table** and **Today's Horse Racing Declaration Table.**

I created a common SQL stored procedure called hr.get_course_wins_flt that would derive the data entity distance wins for a horse. The SQL code snippet below for the procedure will outline how I derived distance wins for a horse.

/****** **Start Of SQL Code Snippet**

```
CREATE PROCEDURE hr.get_course_wins_flt(IN_COURSE VARCHAR(50), IN IN_RACE_TIME

CHAR(5), IN_HORSE VARCHAR(50), IN_DISTANCE CHAR(10), IN_GOING CHAR(5),

IN IN_RACE_DATE DATE, IN IN_CLASS char(5), IN IN_WEIGHT integer, IN IN_AGE

integer, IN IN_BHB char(5) )

for v6 as

select count(*) as distance_wins from Past Results Table where IN_HORSE = horse  and race_type in ( 'AWF',
'FLT') and position in ( '1' ) and

(distance_num(IN_DISTANCE) = distance_num(distance) ) and race_date < IN_RACE_DATE

do

    update generic.dumtab_flt set distance_wins = V6.distance_wins where horse = IN_HORSE and race_date
= IN_RACE_DATE;

end for;--
```

/****** End Of SQL Code Snippet

The parameter IN_DISTANCE is taken from the **Today's Horse Racing Declaration Table** this is the racing distance for today's race and is passed as a parameter to the stored procedure hr.get_course_wins_flt.

The distance is taken from the **Past Results Table.**

race_type specifies the race type we are interested in the past results for a horse 'FLT' or 'AWF'.

The function distance_num() converts the distance from its raw data form i.e. 2m 4f to total furlongs 20 furlongs in this case, this makes querying the database tables easier.

The count(*) as distance_wins is a count of distance wins for a horse in race types 'FLT' and 'AWF' and stored in the derived data entity distance wins.

In the code snippet below you can see a call to the SQL stored procedure hr.get_course_wins_flt for each horse in our **Today's Horse Racing Declaration Table**.

/****** Start Of SQL Code Snippet

```
-- Get Course/Distance/Going Wins

 call hr.get_course_wins_flt(v1.course, v1.race_time, v1.horse, v1.distance, v1.going, v1.race_date, v1.class,
(weight_num(rtrim(v1.weight))), v1.age, v1.jock_club_rating );
```

/****** End Of SQL Code Snippet

In that SQL stored procedure I derive other data entities like course wins, going wins and weight wins for a horse plus many more.

3. **The racing weight difference from its last race and today's race is less than or equal to 0.**

We can derive the weight difference a horse has carried from its last race and today's race. We take the horse last race weight from the and **Past Results Table** and today's race weight for the horse from the **Today's Horse Racing Declaration Table**.

Last weight difference = today's weight – last weight

The data entity today's weight is taken from **Today's Horse Racing Declaration Table**.

The data entity last weight is taken from **Past Results Table** and is the last race the horse has run in.

The above data entities are stored as Character 10 data types so I had to convert this to numeric.

I downloaded and exported the today's and last race weight data in its raw form as 8-12 which is 8 stone 12 pounds and I convert this to total pounds which 8X14 + 12 = 124 pounds this makes the weight difference calculation easier.

4. **The horse's Horse form consistency value is in the top 3 ranking for today's race.**

This is quite simple to derive for this we simply add up the last 3 race positions of a horse. If the horse has fallen or pulled up you can simply ignore that race and look at its next last race or allocate a value of 10 which I explained in detail in the chapter **Derived Data Entities.**

For any given race i.e. today's race say Wolverhampton 4.00 once we have the horse form consistency value for each horse in the race we need to rank these in ascending order. This means the lowest value will be ranked at the top.

So horse A has consistency value of 6 and horse B consistency value of 12 and then horse C has a consistency value 7 then finally horse D has a consistency value of 14 the ranking would be,

Horse A 6

Horse C 7

Horse B 12

Horse D 14

We are only interested in the top 3 rankings which are horse A, horse C and horse B. In SQL query terms this is easy to implement and this derived data is quite important in assessing if a horse is in form.

5. **The horse last race prize money is in the top 3 ranking for today's race.**

The code snippet below outlines how I obtain the last prize for a race a horse competed in. I have also included the code to obtain the 2nd and 3rd last prize as well. I have highlighted in different colours important parts of the code snippet. We are interested in the variable last_prize.

Once we have the race last prize money the horse competed in we rank these in descending order (highest prize money first) and we are only interested in the top 3.

/**** Start Of SQL Code Snippet**

```
for v4 as

    select speed, race_date, integer('0'||CUMLATIVE_LENGTH_BEATEN) as lbtn,  integer(prize1) as last_prize, position, weight, distance,
bhb, class from generic.results where upper(IN_HORSE) = upper(horse) and race_date < IN_RACE_DATE and position not in ( 'P', 'U', 'F', 'S',
'B' ) and race_type in ( 'FLT', 'AWF' ) order by race_date desc fetch first 3 rows only

do


    if IT_COUNT = 1  THEN

        set  w_prize=integer(v4.last_prize);--

            update generic.dumtab_flt set speed=integer(v4.speed), last_class = V4.class, last_prize = w_prize, last_position =
v4.position, last_weight = weight_num(rtrim(v4.weight)), last_distance = distance_num(v4.distance), last_bhb = integer(v4.bhb),
CUM_LBEATEN=v4.lbtn where horse = IN_HORSE and race_date = IN_RACE_DATE;--


    end if;--


    if IT_COUNT = 2  THEN

        set  w_prize=integer(v4.last_prize);--

        update generic.dumtab_flt set speed2=v4.speed, last_class_2 = V4.class, last_prize_2 = w_prize, last_position_2 = v4.position,
last_weight_2 = weight_num(rtrim(v4.weight)), last_distance_2 = distance_num(v4.distance), last_bhb_2 = integer(v4.bhb),
CUM_LBEATEN=v4.lbtn  where horse = IN_HORSE and race_date = IN_RACE_DATE;--

    end if;--


    if IT_COUNT = 3 THEN

        set  w_prize=integer(v4.last_prize);--

        update generic.dumtab_flt set last_class_3 = V4.class, last_prize_3 = w_prize, last_position_3 = v4.position, last_weight_3 =
weight_num(rtrim(v4.weight)), last_distance_3 = distance_num(v4.distance), last_bhb_3 = integer(v4.bhb), CUM_LBEATEN=v4.lbtn  where
horse = IN_HORSE and race_date = IN_RACE_DATE;--

    end if;--

    set IT_COUNT = IT_COUNT + 1;--

end for;--
```

/**** End Of SQL Code Snippet**

6. The average ability is in the top 4 ranking for today's race.

I touched on this earlier in the book this is easy to derive. We are interested in the top 4 starting
with the highest average ability of horse first.

Select sum(Prize1) as ability from past_history_table where horse = 'A Pint Of Bear' and Last Race Position='1'

We could then divide this value of total winning prize money prize1 by the total number of races the horse won to give a value of average winning prize money for the horse. Please see code snippet below to calculate average ability for a horse.

/**** Start Of SQL Code Snippet**

```
-- Total Win Prize and average ability for a horse

for v2 as

    select sum(integer(prize1)) as total_prize, count(*) as num_wins from generic.results where IN_HORSE = horse and position in ( '1' ) and race_type in ( 'FLT', 'AWF' ) and race_date < IN_RACE_DATE

do


    -- Calculate Ability


  if v2.total_prize > 0 then

      set v_ability = v2.total_prize / v2.num_wins;--

        set v_ability_perc = v_ability / 100;--

    end if;--

    update generic.dumtab_flt set total_win_prize = V2.total_prize, num_wins = v2.num_wins, ability = v_ability, ability_perc = v_ability_perc where horse = IN_HORSE and race_date = IN_RACE_DATE;--


end for;--
```

/**** End Of SQL Code Snippet**

We are interested in the variable v_ability.

Reporting Potential Horse Selections For A Bet

Now we have derived our data we can now select the best horses for potential bets. Please see code snippet below that will query the derived data entity table grfltall2 and dumtab_flt_proto for flat and all weather racing.

Table grfltall2 contains ranking data like last prize ranking or consistent horse form rank etc. I added this database table to make processing of rankings for ability, consistency value and last race prize easier.

Table dumtab_flt_proto contains derived data like days last run for a horse or ability of a horse etc.

These database tables are also used for modelling past results as I create duplicate tables for archiving under a different database schema.

I have highlighted in yellow key columns which we can pattern match for.

/**** Start Of SQL Code Snippet**

```
select substr(A1.race_time,1,5) as race_time, A2.todays_prize/100 as tprize, A2.todays_distance as td, A2.last_distance as ld,
A2.last_position as pos1, substr(A1.course,1,10) as course, substr(A1.horse,1,25) as horse,
A2.ability_perc as ab,
case when ( A2.last_position is not null and A2.last_position in ( '1', '2', '3', '4', '5', '6', '7', '8', '9', '10', '11', '12', '13', '14', '15', '16', '17', '18',
'19', '20' ) and A2.last_position_2 is not null and A2.last_position_2 in ( '1', '2', '3', '4', '5', '6', '7', '8', '9', '10', '11', '12', '13', '14', '15', '16',
'17', '18', '19', '20' ) and  A2.last_position_3 in ( '1', '2', '3', '4', '5', '6', '7', '8', '9', '10', '11', '12', '13', '14', '15', '16', '17', '18', '19', '20' ) and
A2.last_position_3 is not null ) then
( integer(A2.last_position)+integer(A2.last_position_2)+integer(A2.last_position_3)) else A2.consist end as consist,

(A2.last_prize/100),

integer(A2.jock_club_rating) as bhb,

a2.todays_weight-A2.last_weight as wdiff,

a2.total_runs,

A2.days_last_run dlr,

case when A2.total_runs<13 then 'TR+' else ' ' end,
case when A2.last_position in ( '1', '2' ) then 'X+' else ' ' end ,
case when A1.consist_rank<=3 then 'C+' else ' ' end,
case when A1.ability_rank<=4 then 'A+' else ' ' end,
case when A1.lp1_rank<=3 then 'L+' else ' ' end,
case when A2.course_wins>0 then 'CW+' else ' ' end,
case when A2.distance_wins>0 then 'DW+' else ' ' end ,
case when A2.days_last_run<=50 then 'DLR+' else ' ' end ,
case when A1.bhb_rank<=2 then 'B+' else ' ' end

from archive.grfltall2 A1, archive.dumtab_flt_proto A2

where A1.race_date=IN_RACE_DATE and A1.race_date=A2.race_date and A1.horse=A2.horse and A1.race_time=A2.race_time and
A1.course=A2.course
and hand=IN_HAND
and A2.todays_class in ( '1', '2', '3', '4', '5', '6' )

order by A2.race_date, A2.todays_prize desc, A1.course, A2.RACE_TIME, ( A2.last_prize/100 ) desc, integer(A2.jock_club_rating) desc
```

/**** End Of SQL Code Snippet**

The above reporting SQL uses our **Today's Horse Racing Declaration Table** and **Derived Data Tables.**

Report 1   Race Date 7th June 2021 For UK Handicap Horse Races Only.

The columns in the report starting from left to right are:-

Race Time
Race Prize or penalty value (divided by 100)
Today's race distance
Last Race Distance
Last Race Position
Course
Horse
Horses Average Ability
Horse form consistency value
Last race prize (divided by 100)
Horses BHB rating (Official rating)
Weight difference (today's race weight-last race weight)
Total races run for the horse
Days last run for the horse
TR+ Total runs flag
X+ Last position flag
C+ Consistency form value ranking flag
A+ Ability ranking flag
L+ Last prize ranking flag
CW+ Course wins flag
DW+ Distance wins flag
DLR+ Days horse last run flag
B+ BHB Rating ranking flag

Race Time	Prize/100	Today Dist	Last Dist	Last Pos	Course	Horse	Avg Ability	Consistency	Last Prize/100	BHB	Weight Diff	Total Races	Days Last Run	Flags
6-45	96	12	10	5	PONTEFRACT	Restorer	129	14	103	97	7	43	31	C+ A+ L+ DW+ DLR+ B+
6-45	96	12	14	1	PONTEFRACT	A Star Above	57	13	103	89	3	9	24	TR+ X+ C+ A+ L+ DW+ DLR+
6-30	60	5	5	2	WINDSOR	Thegreatestshowman	56	8	74	82	12	40	130	X+ C+ A+ L+ DW+
8-45	58	6	6	1	PONTEFRACT	Excel Power	35	3	43	88	0	4	13	TR+ X+ C+ A+ L+ DW+ DLR+ B+
8-45	58	6	6	3	PONTEFRACT	Mitrosonfire	34	13	43	75	-2	8	13	TR+ C+ A+ L+ DW+ DLR+
8-45	58	6	6	1	PONTEFRACT	Bergerac	29	9	29	87	-3	6	40	TR+ X+ C+ A+ L+ CW+ DW+ DLR+ B+
8-15	44	17	16	3	PONTEFRACT	Arabescato	33	10	43	75	0	18	45	C+ A+ L+ CW+ DLR+ B+
8-15	44	17	16	10	PONTEFRACT	Warranty	27	13	28	67	-11	8	20	TR+ C+ A+ L+ DLR+
2-00	43	10	10	4	LEICESTER	Oz Legend	40	8	257	82	16	4	23	TR+ C+ A+ L+ DLR+
2-00	43	10	10	1	LEICESTER	No Recollection	44	8	44	85	0	6	36	TR+ X+ C+ A+ L+ DW+ DLR+ B+

Time				Course	Horse								Flags
2-00	43	10	11 7	LEICESTER	Otyrar	31	10	43	83	-1	5	24	TR+ C+ A+ L+ DW+ DLR+ B+
3-30	43	7	8 6	LEICESTER	Mr Tyrrell	45	14	34	74	-7	39	175	C+ A+ L+
7-00	43	11	12 4	WINDSOR	Miss Mulligan	52	9	118	80	4	8	16	TR+ C+ A+ L+ CW+ DLR+
7-00	43	11	16 5	WINDSOR	Summeronsevenhills	45	10	64	87	1	15	31	C+ A+ L+ DLR+ B+
7-00	43	11	12 3	WINDSOR	Goldie Hawk	44	6	59	80	6	7	19	TR+ C+ A+ L+ DLR+
6-15	29	6	7 3	PONTEFRACT	Magical Effect	44	8	51	72	-8	55	16	C+ A+ L+ CW+ DW+ DLR+ B+
6-15	29	6	6 3	PONTEFRACT	Final Frontier	150	12	44	61	15	31	40	C+ A+ L+ DW+ DLR+
5-30	28	5	5 5	WINDSOR	Hotalena	29	8	48	67	-4	18	17	C+ A+ L+ DW+ DLR+
8-00	28	5	5 5	WINDSOR	Buy Me Back	33	11	28	70	-1	19	18	C+ A+ L+ DW+ DLR+ B+
8-00	28	5	6 2	WINDSOR	Clashaniska	30	4	27	60	-6	16	82	X+ C+ A+ L+
7-45	27	10	10 2	PONTEFRACT	Bit Of A Quirke	44	5	47	64	12	44	9	X+ C+ A+ L+ DW+ DLR+
7-45	27	10	10 12	PONTEFRACT	Lexington Warfare	27	17	28	66	6	14	13	C+ A+ L+ DLR+ B+
4-00	23	7	8 4	LEICESTER	Sir Taweel	23	14	28	62	6	6	7	TR+ C+ A+ L+ DLR+
4-45	23	5	5 4	LINGFIELD	Aleef	77	12	23	63	-6	57	12	C+ A+ L+ DW+ DLR+ B+
1-45	23	12	11 1	LINGFIELD	Yagan	23	16	23	58	7	5	10	TR+ X+ C+ A+ L+ DLR+
2-45	23	8	9 10	LINGFIELD	Trepidation	27	14	23	57	2	13	18	C+ A+ L+ DW+ DLR+ B+
2-45	23	8	12 6	LINGFIELD	Compass Point	30	10	23	55	1	41	18	C+ A+ L+ CW+ DW+ DLR+

The first filter I apply to this report is as follows this will reduce the number of possible bets considerably. I am only looking for patterns C+ A+ and L+ for horses to qualify.

C+ = **The horse's Horse form consistency value is in the top 3 ranking for today's race.**

A+ = **The average ability is in the top 4 ranking for today's race.**

L+ = **The horse last race prize money is in the top 3 ranking for today's race.**

Report 2 Race Date 7ᵗʰ June 2021

Using the same **Report 1** I have added an extra condition in the SQL query where Last weight difference is less than or equal to 0 which reduces the number of horses again. This condition satisfies **The racing weight difference from its last race and today's race is less than or equal to 0.**

and A2.todays_weight-A2.last_weight<=0

8-45	58	6	6 3	PONTEFRACT	Mitrosonfire		34	13	43	75	-2	8	13 TR+	C+ A+
L+	DW+ DLR+													
8-45	58	6	6 1	PONTEFRACT	Bergerac		29	9	29	87	-3	6	40 TR+ X+ C+ A+ L+	
CW+ DW+ DLR+ B+														
8-15	44	17	16 10	PONTEFRACT	Warranty		27	13	28	67	-11	8	20 TR+ C+ A+	
L+	DLR+													
2-00	43	10	11 7	LEICESTER	Otyrar	31	10	43	83	-1	5	24 TR+ C+ A+ L+		
DW+ DLR+ B+														
3-30	43	7	8 6	LEICESTER	Mr Tyrrell	45	14	34	74	-7	39	175 C+ A+ L+		
6-15	29	6	7 3	PONTEFRACT	Magical Effect		44	8	51	72	-8	55	16 C+ A+ L+	
CW+ DW+ DLR+ B+														
5-30	28	5	5 5	WINDSOR	Hotalena	29	8	48	67	-4	18	17 C+ A+ L+		
DW+ DLR+														
8-00	28	5	5 5	WINDSOR	Buy Me Back		33	11	28	70	-1	19	18 C+ A+ L+	
DW+ DLR+ B+														
8-00	28	5	6 2	WINDSOR	Clashaniska		30	4	27	60	-6	16	82 X+ C+ A+ L+	
4-45	23	5	5 4	LINGFIELD	Aleef	77	12	23	63	-6	57	12 C+ A+ L+		
DW+ DLR+ B+														

Report 3 Race Date 7th June 2021

Now using **Report 2** above I have now added two more conditions to the SQL query this reduces yet again the number of selections in the report.

Distance Wins DW+

Days The Horse Last Run DLR+

I have highlighted the winners that day in green this is pretty good and it's all automated!

8-45	58	6	6 3	PONTEFRACT	Mitrosonfire		34	13	43	75	-2	8	13 TR+	C+ A+
L+	DW+ DLR+													
8-45	58	6	6 1	PONTEFRACT	Bergerac		29	9	29	87	-3	6	40 TR+ X+ C+ A+ L+	
CW+ DW+ DLR+ B+														
2-00	43	10	11 7	LEICESTER	Otyrar	31	10	43	83	-1	5	24 TR+ C+ A+ L+		
DW+ DLR+ B+														
6-15	29	6	7 3	PONTEFRACT	Magical Effect		44	8	51	72	-8	55	16 C+ A+ L+	
CW+ DW+ DLR+ B+														
5-30	28	5	5 5	WINDSOR	Hotalena	29	8	48	67	-4	18	17 C+ A+ L+		
DW+ DLR+														
8-00	28	5	5 5	WINDSOR	Buy Me Back		33	11	28	70	-1	19	18 C+ A+ L+	
DW+ DLR+ B+														
4-45	23	5	5 4	LINGFIELD	Aleef	77	12	23	63	-6	57	12 C+ A+ L+		
DW+ DLR+ B+														

Mitrosonfire   Won 7/2

Hotalena Won 9/1

Buy Me Back Won 9/2

Aleef Won 12/1

This was a great days racing and very profitable I like looking for the golden nuggets this horse racing system produces and I am very selective. This horse racing system is very simple I have other systems which are also automatic but look at different angles on racing and these are explained in my other books.

Securing Your Database And Tables

I strongly recommend you backup up your database tables and code as you will get some hardware failure in the future. I backup my system every week automatically without failure. I also clone my hard drive to an external drive in case I lose the lot. This happened to me a few years ago and I recovered the system very quickly.

Conclusions.

After you have read my book you might think this a great deal of work to do, yes it is but once you have your UK horse racing system it certainly makes life easier in the future picking winning horses.

Automatic systems save you a great deal of time trawling through horse form but I do confess I always make the final decision on the horses it produces.

Consultant Services

I have certainly learned a great deal around automatic horse racing system implementation. I know the pitfalls and what will save you time and your money. I offer my services for a fixed rate, I have over 25 years I.T experience and 30 years betting and trading on horses. If you are interested in using my services please feel free to email me at

vanderwheil6@gmail.com

Printed in Great Britain
by Amazon

41054222R00025